More praise for *Poems in a Time of Grief*

"Writing this on the first anniversary of my father's death,
I am acquainted with grief. Each death is unique, and yet,
each is universal. G. Greene's rhyming, rhythmic, and free verse
expressions are a raw, honest, "unapologetically sentimental"
gift to us all, given with the hope that his experience,
shared, will help others feel less alone."

— C.J. King, MFA–Creative Writing, and author of
*Four Marys and a Jessie: The Story of the Lincoln Women*

"In this book, G. Greene gives us the best and the worst
of life. Penned after his wife died, his poems are heartbreaking,
an outpouring of grief at its most raw. But this testament
to great love is a reminder that life can offer joy as well
as sorrow. That this is both a source of solace and pain
is among the most profound of truths."

— Dr. Anne Buchanan, Adjunct Research Professor of Anthropology,
Pennsylvania State University, coauthor of
*The Mermaid's Tale: Four Billion Years of Evolution*

# poems in a time of grief

G. Greene

Website: poemsinatimeofgrief.com

Ordering Information:
For details, contact poemsinatimeofgrief@gmail.com

Print ISBN: 978-1-09833-252-5
eBook ISBN: 978-1-09833-253-2

Cover Image by G. Greene
Cover and Interior Design by David Provolo
Editing by Eric Muhr



Printed in the United States of America

First Edition

*For Jean,*

*the owner of my heart.*

*This is for you.*

# foreword

This isn't a book written for lovers of poetry.

This is a book of poetry written for those grieving a personal loss, by someone who was and is grieving. In my case, my grief is for my wife, my partner and love for several decades before she was taken by a devastating autoimmune neurological disease that remained undiagnosed and virtually untreatable. I don't go into the details of that herein because this isn't the story of her medical odyssey but rather, my attempt to deal with her death and reconcile myself to a life without her, which has been challenging beyond description. It's a process that continues to this day.

If you dislike sentiment in poetry (and it has been suggested to me that sentimentality has little place in poetry) then I must apologize in advance because many of the poems herein are nakedly and unapologetically sentimental. They are hardly the stuff of greeting card verse, but they speak of love, both directly and obliquely, and unashamedly in all instances.

With those disclaimers in place, a little about me:

I've always enjoyed writing, but my focus prior to my wife's passing, at least in terms of poetry, was typically satire, song parodies, and the like, or the occasional humorous birthday poem for friends.

I'd really never written a word of "serious" poetry, whatever definition one chooses to use for that, until several months after my wife's death. In an early visit with a grief therapist, they described my situation as living in a world of wrong, which sparked the first poem simply because I thought it an apt description of my circumstance. So I wrote and edited "World of Wrong," then gave it no more thought.

This volume began its gestation in earnest when I ignored my therapist's advice to have a plan in place for the first significant holiday I'd be spending alone after my wife died, which, in my case, happened to be Memorial Day 2019. I thought, "Well, that was never a significant holiday for us, so I'll be fine." So, with no plan in place I quite predictably ended up the furthest thing from fine that very, very long weekend. In the accompanying emotional turmoil, the very first poem borne of pain came out in a surprised rush over the holiday weekend.

Once the figurative emotional dam had been breached, the rest of these poems followed, sometimes several a week, sometimes just one over several weeks. The act of writing them became an integral part of my grieving process as well as a way to communicate to friends and family how I was feeling long beyond the point in time where such conversations might have been welcomed or comfortable for anyone involved, myself included.

As the poems piled up, it was suggested to me that, assembled into a slim volume, they might provide some relief or release or comfort to others in similar circumstances, whether grieving a spouse, parent, sibling, child, friend or lover — anyone trying to cope with grief due to the loss of a loved one.

So the idea was born to assemble enough pieces to fill a small volume and put them out in the world as expressions of grief in poetic form that might provide some insight or respite for others, even if only to say that there's someone out here who has perhaps shared some of the same feelings and reactions the reader might be going through.

Writing this book certainly wasn't a commercial enterprise, as I expect it will cost me more financially and emotionally than it could possibly return. In the end, I'll call it a success if just one person receives some comfort from it. If that should happen, it will have been worth the effort of publication.

These poems are presented in the order in which they were written, over a period of approximately a year. I may have matured during that time, even if only just a little, in terms of my writing, and hopefully some scant evidence of that comes through here. That's another way of saying, if the first few hold little appeal, hang in there, there are, I think, better ones coming.

To any serious poets among my hoped-for readers, I suffer from no delusion that this tome somehow makes me a poet. I don't believe it does. To the skilled, practiced, and published poets of the world, these pieces may well be fraught with error and naivete or violate some real or customary standards. Though I hold both undergraduate and graduate degrees, I've had little exposure in my life to poetry and crafting poems.

I pointedly avoided reading other author's poetry

when this volume began to take shape because I didn't want my efforts to end up imitating other poets, other poems, or styles of writing, however unintentionally. (There are, however, a few references to the work of poets I recall from my school years.) I did attend a single, brief, and valuable writer's workshop on revising and editing one's own poems. That aside, I accept responsibility for whatever flaws or lapses occur in these pages.

I haven't tried, as I feel ill-equipped to do so, to compose poetry that might stand some test of time, or not suffer by comparison to more schooled, skilled, or literate poets. (Which is not to say that I haven't labored over these compositions. I absolutely have.) I've tried simply to express my grief and work through my subsequent depression, using poetry as the form, and offer it here in the hope that it might proffer a moment's catharsis for people in similar circumstances. If a reader were to feel a little less alone in their grief because of something they read here, that would be very humbling and gratifying to me.

In the end, I've said what I needed to say through my writing. As for everything else, I'll let these poems speak for themselves, for me, and for my beloved and brilliant wife, Jean.

G. Greene

# dedications

There are a number of people without whom this book would never have seen the light, so in a way, this is their fault. (Kidding.) No importance should be attached to the order herein, as someone had to be first, and someone had to be last. I hope I didn't leave anyone out, and if I did, I can only apologize. So here goes nothing.

Donna, you appeared as a friend just when a friend had never been more needed. Thank you so very much. I will never forget how much you did to help Jean throughout the last months of her ordeal. She didn't know you long, but she loved you dearly.

Eileen, Greg, and Lauri — thanks for being my second family. Thanks for the visits and e-mails, the criticism and encouragement. Thanks for everything. Much love.

Barb, you amaze me. If I could be half as good a friend to a third as many people, I'd be quite happy. Your steadfast support has been so important. I just don't have the words to thank you, "Big Sis."

Michael, nearly fifty years of friendship have seen us both through some hard times. This is the hardest time of all for me, and without you there, I'm not sure how it would have turned out. Thank you, my friend.

Pierre and Lucille, neighbors by chance, but friends by choice. Thank you for your love, support, walks, and kindness (and all the muffins) through this terrible time, even as you have endured your own trials.

Liz, unfortunately you traveled down this road ahead of me. Your sharing your experience helped me with my own. Thank you.

Sue — Hey, Cuz'. Thanks for being one of my faithful (and gentle) readers while these poems took shape. Your kindness and support meant the world to me. When others fell away, you hung in there. Thank you.

Kim, many thanks for your enthusiastic support and steadfast encouragement. Most of all, thank you for being Jeannie's friend, and mine.

To anyone reading this book — thank you. Writing it helped me, a lot. I hope it helps you, if only a little, to read it.

And of course, to my beloved Jeannie. Words fail me, as they did so frequently in my attempts at capturing my thoughts. Thank you for being so resolute in getting my attention, when I was so oblivious, and ultimately rescuing me from myself. Thank you for your humor, your compassion, your kindness, your faith, and your boundless, relentless optimism. Thank you for your valor in suffering through a malady you never deserved, never once questioning why it had to be that way. You set an example that I would be proud to achieve when the time comes, if only I had your strength. Thank you for your modesty, your brilliance, your intelligence. Thank you for slowing me down and teaching me how to take it easy, or at least easier. Thank you for learning how to ski, for suggesting the cabin we built and loved, and for all the friends you brought into our life when my glib tongue and unpersuasive manner might have driven them off. Thank you for the thousands of memories of a life I couldn't have dreamed of before you came along and set your cap for me. Thank you for being my friend, my lover, my teacher, my example. Life is so much emptier without you, but I'm hanging on, Honey, in the hope that you were right about what happens next, so thank you for your belief. Thank you for letting me protect you as best I could and for letting me think you needed protecting. A final confession: I lied when I said I'd love, honor, and cherish you until death do us part. Though we're parted, none of that has changed. Maybe one day I'll get to show you.

G

# world of wrong

Welcome to your World of Wrong,
where everyone you loved is gone;
sister, brother, parents, wife,
bequeath you to a singular life.

The World of Wrong's a hollow place,
where you dwell, submerged, in empty space,
a realm once brimming with love and light,
now less like day, more like night.

All can see, but few dare speak
because your wrong world looks so bleak.
If given voice, the pain laid bare,
they fear they'd find they've joined you there.

So they talk about nothing, and hope you feel better,
wishing their best, but not really ever
discussing the loss that suffuses your mind,
for if they looked closely, perhaps they might find

they, too, are destined for a wrongful place,
a world bereft, of deep malaise,
whether bonded there by fateful strife,
or they, themselves, pass from this life,
and gain entry to the World of Wrong,
where everyone they loved — is gone.

— 5/11/19

# bargaining

Here is my promise, if only you'll stay,
if you'll hold on each morning for just one more day:
More ice cream than your tummy can hold,
and a love more precious than silver or gold,
with kisses in the morning,
and a matinee every day,
that's what I promise, if only you'll stay.

The doctors don't really know what to do,
so many tests, and still there's no clue,
but if you swear to ignore all of their warnings,
I'll make every day your own Christmas morning,
or pull a star down with a fine silken rope,
whatever you want, just give me hope
that you'll stay by my side, now and forever,
just say you won't leave me, and remain as my lover.

Did I mention the marigolds and daisies and roses?
We'll live with flowers up to our noses,
and if, by chance, they should make you sneeze,
I'll conjure up a loving breeze

to blow away the dust and the pollen
so you'll know in your heart that my heart is swollen
with love for you, and that it would be a lie,
if I say it won't break if you should die.

So here is my promise, if only you'll stay -
I'll love you like each day is our very last day,
then someday, perhaps, when fate insists,
we'll pass, together, into the mists
of whatever awaits us in the hereafter,
perhaps to live on in your light and your laughter.

But now, it seems, you were forced to leave,
and I, alone, am left to grieve
a love that will last all through the ages,
until last words are written on very last pages.
I know that you were compelled to go,
for reasons that I'll never know,
so I'll love you still, even though I can't follow,
and I'm forced to stay here and live with the hollow
place in my chest where my heart used to dwell,
to exist, alone, in my own private Hell,
recalling the times we laughed and we played,
and know we'd play still, if you could have stayed.

— 5/27/19

# denial

No, no, no — you just can't be gone,
that would be awful, and so very wrong.
Just stop — please stop — and think for a minute;
what would the world be without both of us in it?
It wouldn't make sense, me without you,
so you can't be gone, I won't accept that it's true.

Who would answer when I call your pet name,
and how could we play all of our games?
Without you here, the days would be long,
the nights never-ending, and lacking a dawn
to welcome the day with you at its center,
simply your presence making it better.

So you just can't be gone,
for without you there's no me,
and the world as I know it would just cease to be
the kind of place I would want to live in,
and feel more like some joyless prison,
the sunless days, cloying and empty,
like life in some cloistered abbey

where the penitents are bound never to speak,
consumed by the silence until their spirits break.

So wherever you're hiding, whatever you're up to,
please come out, and let me forgive you,
and while you revel in your clever prank,
just don't expect that I'm going to thank
you for scaring me so, for making me worry,
just please come out now, and say that you're sorry.

Something in my eyes is making them burn,
and it feels like we've taken a really bad turn,
so, please, won't you help me? Don't leave me like this,
this just isn't funny, and I'm starting to miss
the sound of your voice, the music in your laugh,
because you're not just a part of me,
you're far more than half,
and if you don't return soon,
we won't finish our song,
so it just can't be true.
You just can't be gone.

— 6/13/19

# penance

Waking each day,
before rising,

I don my grief,
a coat of thorns that stab at every turn,

still damp with yesterday's tears,
lined with regret,

pockets full of memories,
the sagging, sodden weight of it

hampering every step,
clinging like a shroud until

the mourning moon brings fretful sleep
and it's closeted once again,

limp and unfulfilled,
awaiting the dawn.

— 6/13/19

# someone

I miss being someone
you could ask for anything,
even as you gave me everything.
Your needing me,
when I need you more,
now our time is over.
Your loving smile,
the source of my own,
and our days together
as I stumble on alone.
Talking with you,
as I strain to hear your voice
in the unimaginable silence.
I miss your generous, delighted laugh,
and I'm spent with crying
each time I remember,
now that I'm no one,
how I loved
being your someone.

— 6/18/19

# anniversary

Death knows me,
seeking my union
many times but
always balking,
pulling the hook,
a fish too small to gut.
Patient;
watchful;
waiting.
Death returned,
not for me,
but for you,
knowing it had found
something, the one thing,
more precious to me than life,
more awful than dying,
ripening me for the taking
next time, full grown,
baptized, fattened on heartbreak,
seeking the lure,
yearning for the fire.

— 6/23/19

# Haiku – June 2019

Forty years, one love,
gone now for eternity.
My soul is shattered.

I stand at your grave
and think of nothing more than
your bright morning smile.

Lost along our road,
I am unable to find
a path that joins yours.

An endless riddle,
no answer, no solution;
once alive, now not.

No reason, no crime,
taken by an unknown scourge,
no one can say how.

Time — the balm for wounds.
But this is no mere wound — this
is death cheating life.

A moment in time,
your heart finally quieted.
We died together.

How could one moment,
so stark, brief, peaceful, quiet,
cause such boundless pain?

As a tree grips fast
its earthen surround, my heart
holds the thought of you.

Called by your God, could
he not have left you with me,
and made another?

As the light faded,
your heart took flight to heaven;
my heart fell to earth.

A light extinguished,
a laugh like falling water
flows beyond hearing.

One gone, one remains,
no question of fair, not fair.
Simply what happened.

Death hides in shadow,
a sleeping cat in the night,
when it rouses, strikes.

Grief, intimate fog,
emotion that envelops
and smothers this life.

Where does love go when
its living vessel departs,
never to return?

An errant, false gene
began a storm that ended
all that came before.

I would follow you,
if I knew where you have gone.
Your trail is bare, lost.

# memory

There is now,
moment by moment,
in endless succession
or memory,
life's past procession.
Now is rendered endless pain,
memory where you live still,
and I would choose to live again.

— 7/19/19

# paintings

Your paintings illuminating every wall,
as I enter, I hear your call,
your laughter echoing in the silent air,
while wishful eyes still see you here.

My spirit falters when I pause to wonder
at all our years, gone forever.
We thought we still had time, but no,
you were christened and compelled to go.

So I linger now, a life confined
to living alone as sadness defined,
life's purpose relinquished without you here,
empty arms aching to draw you near.

In the ruined hours of every night,
I wonder, why keep at the fight?
Where's the meaning in fumbling on,
life's melody silenced, a beggared song?

For in the end, the end's the same,
and life's revealed a zero-sum game,
all players play a single round,
none win, none lose; all go to ground.

— 7/20/19

# the singer

On the sidewalk,
his concrete stage,
a broken singer, a battered speaker,
limited engagement,
songs of loss and heartbreak,
exposing his soul for tips,
saving for a trip to Olympus,
to see where the gods used to live.

— 7/20/19

# spooky action at a distance

We were bound together in arguable death
eons before we ever drew breath,
pre-atomic bits of a vanished singularity,
a singular, unreasonable, extraordinary rarity,
all that was then or would forever be possible,
densely confined, universally improbable.

Instantly expelled at the genesis of everything,
we transited time far beyond reasoning,
saw galaxies created, stars born,
worlds destroyed, the cosmos form,
black holes, nebulae, galactic collisions,
abiding nature's quantum indecisions.

The seeds of our souls, dormant at the start,
through all space and time, never apart,
finally, to Earth, a home to take shape in,
adapting, evolving, to at last become human.
Billions more years down an infinite path,
you and I, alive, creation's aftermath.

Ordained from the start, our lives coincided,
finding consummate love until grim death divided
me from you, and you from our world,
to return to the stars from which we were hurled,
where fate could allege the end of our story,
to be mined only once from time's infinite quarry.

Logic would proclaim this grief's futile lament,
a promise to you borne solely from torment,
but whatever can happen will happen, it is said,
and so I declaim with my heart and my head:
amidst endless stars, I found you on this earthly plane,
and I swear by those stars, I'll find you again.

— 7/24/19

# essence

A hug

warmer than laundry fresh from the dryer.

A smile

sweeter than sugar on snow.

A laugh

brighter than sun on the water.

A heart

more generous than I'd ever known.

A life

filled to the brim with the joy of living.

A spirit

fulfilled by the satisfaction of giving.

A light

to brighten the darkest of mornings.

Gone now,

to witness eternity's dawning.

— 7/26/19

# hero

All I ever wanted was to be your hero,
from our very first meeting, just to be near you,
to know you, hold you, never be apart
while we found a home in each other's hearts,
to spend our lives together, go different places,
and be the one who knew all of your faces,
the happy, the sad, the impatient ones, too,
then be the one who knew just what to do
to make you feel better, tease out your laughter,
or help dry your tears and comfort you after.
You knew I was there if you needed support,
but only as the last resort,
as we both knew, whatever came your way,
you often didn't need me to help save the day,
while, in kindness, you allowed me my fantasy,
though I needed you as much as you needed me.
Now you're gone, and I've no role to play,
no steed to mount, no beast I can slay,
just living each moment, wearied and haggard,
all effort in vain, heart full of daggers,
my soul on offer if it would bring you home
from wherever your soul has gone now to roam.

— 8/22/19

# these days

In the shower,
I can't feel the tears.
In my sleep,
I don't feel the fear.
In the dark,
I can't see I'm alone.
In our house,
I don't feel at home.
In the world,
I can't feel the grace.
In my grief,
I don't accept our fate.
In my thoughts,
I can't deny the proof.
In my heart,
I don't believe the truth.
In my life,
I don't know how to care.
In my dreams,
I can't feel you near.
In the moment,
I can't face the climb.

In the future,
I don't see being fine.
In the end,
I can't bear the pain.
In the quietus,
will we embrace again?

— 8/24/19

# yesterday's dream

Yesterday, arriving home,
opening the door,
hearing the television
*(I thought I — didn't I turn it off?)*
playing your favorite channel,
my mind, lying in wait,
quicker than I could think,
slipped its leash
and pounced on the forsaken wish.
*(It was a nightmare! She's here!)*
Though I knew, even as I looked,
you wouldn't — couldn't — be there,
nothing could prise my mind from its quarry,
*(She's back! Go and see! Go!)*
and in the looking
I died again, and in the dying
was your last breath, my lost hope.
As I woke into the nightmare again today,
desolate, adrenalized tears sliding down my face,
I thought,
*Please, God — not another.*

— 8/29/19

# for my mom, Lillian

She rises, tentatively.
Her somnolent heart,
startled into action,
attempts a disorganized rally.
Ancient blood unpressured,
floor rolling beneath her,
she sinks back into her chair,
waits for the fog to recede.
Insufficiently daunted,
survivor of previous squalls,
too soon, another tremulous effort,
victorious, but only just.
Unsteady, stubbornly confident,
she tacks arthritically to the landing.
The powered chair, grumbling,
doggedly lifts her up,
diffident heart granted brief reprieve,
a moment to marshal.
Summiting, she turns and rises,
heedless of the imminent tempest.
A hesitant step,
then another,

consciousness ebbing away
as a second dusk descends.
Caught now,
away from safe harbor,
full in the storm,
heart swooning, nadir breached,
she falls forward,
protective instincts unanswered,
no call to arms,
undefended.
Dreamily accelerating,
she swims into the cataract,
her claim to life resigned,
a casualty of persistence,
anointed by the rising floor
as it rushes up to embrace her
and take her home.

— 9/1/19

# back where it starts

Every day is the same,
every day there's the pain.
Eyes open, something's wrong,
the mind reboots:
< *she's gone* >
Reflexive tears, a punch in the heart
negating the day, another null start,
time ceases flight, the hours mull on,
the world's just the same, except it's all wrong.
Life keeps spinning; I impersonate my part,
lungs keep expanding, but for my heart
another year or a thousand, one and the same,
just more riven days to live with the pain.

— 9/11/19

# good night, my love

Each night,
I say good night to your picture,
with nowhere to turn,
not to drink or to scripture,
to render the anodyne lost lovers seek,
the faith to keep on, the will to proceed,
to be the person I wanted to be for you,
to live the love that would never leave for you.
Your dying took more than I knew I possessed,
bonded me to a realm of grief without rest where
I've tried medication, talk, this verse,
but it seems I'm designed to live out the worst
of loving profoundly, deeply, completely,
forfeit everything that used to complete me,
like digging a tunnel that collapses behind you,
still digging, still seeking a light that might blind you,
the only paths open to bear down and go through,
or abide underground and remain lost
without you.

— 9/12/19

# questions

Can't outrun it,
can't outthink it,
can't outsleep it,
can't outdrink it.

Can't let it in,
can't get it out,
can't let it go,
can't live without.

Can't move forward,
can't go back,
can't replace it,
can't stand the lack.

Where are you now,
and why can't I go?
Will I ever have peace,
and how would I know?

— 9/12/19

# time, the thief

All the good days live in the past,
life itself not meant to last,
no path forward, no way back,
living defined by what it lacks,
commitments made, promises kept,
your life was stolen, Jesus wept,
wrongs left unsettled, debts unpaid,
justice denied 'till judgement day
renders the lesson for both lord and knave
what death can't teach from beyond the grave,
that time itself, the perpetual thief,
dispenses all full measure of grief.

— 9/16/19

# cookie jar

On our counter,
a cookie jar,
a stylized, hot red,
hot rod convertible.
Visitors often remark,
"That's really cute!"
They don't know
it was your first birthday gift to me.
They don't know
we were vacationing on the Cape and,
wandering through a shop,
I saw it, loved it,
but it was too expensive, too extravagant.
They don't know
the very next week,
you took a day off work,
drove to Hyannis and back,
four hundred miles,
to buy it for me.
They don't know
you didn't remember what shop it was in,
so you made your way

in and out of every shop,
searching until you found it.
They don't know
how carefully you brought it home,
tenderly wrapped and hid it,
and waited impatiently for the big day,
fairly bursting with anticipation,
delighted as a child,
barely able to restrain yourself,
thrilled with your secret,
bright as a star, radiant with love.
They don't know
that when I opened it,
I grasped at once the entirety of it;
what you had done, what it meant,
the idea, the plan, the effort,
what you wanted to say,
and within that singular knowing,
through grateful tears,
fell in love with you again,
not for the gift of the little hot rod cookie jar,
but for the gift of you.
It has never held a cookie,
but it has always held two hearts,

bonded in love, leavened by time.
Now you're gone and someday,
when I've left to find you,
it will just be a cookie jar again.
But for now,
for me,
it's everything.

— 9/12/19

# is, is not

She is not ashes,
though that is what remains.
She is not gentle birdsong
or anything else so pedestrian
as the caress of moonlight
on a warm summer lake
or the susurrus of stars
in a frozen winter's midnight sky.
She is dark energy,
postulated, yet unseen,
existing in a realm where quanta
loom larger than Everest,
suspended in a superposition of states,
living and not, until one looks,
and then she is both;
or one;
or neither.
She compels
the irresistible force,
commands
the immovable object,
channels

a magnetism of all things,
not iron alone.
She is entropy,
the inherited disorder
of a world she no longer inhabits,
or cares to be in.
She is not $E=mc^2$,
but caresses its inspiration,
mass and light, interchangeable,
both particle and wave.
She is not ashes,
though that is what remains.
She is everywhere,
she is timeless,
but she is not here,
not now.

— 9/20/19

# diving

Am I okay?
I am not.
God, I would settle for okay
any of these sunken days
when I recall before,
our life,
in a placid sea of contentment
so deep that a diving bell,
patiently machined from a block
of the strongest metal,
wouldn't see you to the bottom of it
before you were crushed
by the light surrounding you.
Yet that's where we lived,
happily tethered, unscathed,
free to come and go,
no need to decompress.
Without you,
I've drifted too deep,
the surface so far above,
air running low,

nitrogen boiling my blood,
light waning,
as darkness drapes the sky.

— 10/4/19

# alone

There is "alone,"
as in they're not here,
but they'll be back, or
perhaps, they exist in the world,
just not in yours.
Then there is "alone,"
as in, they were here
but will never be here again,
no matter what you believe in,
what you would sacrifice,
which god you pray to or deny.
An alone where the borderline
between you and the world,
once extending out from your soul to enfold them,
contain them as you contain yourself,
has receded,
bounded now only by your skin;
your consciousness shrink-wrapped,
aware only of your brine-soaked emotions
and desiccated heart.
That is the alone confronted
from this side of the divide,

the alone that terrifies by *not*
going bump in the night,
the alone of a silence found only
between the galaxies of ourselves.

— 10/10/19

# drowning

Drowning
in a sea of air,
falling,
seated in a chair,
all alone
in every crowd,
sad,
too sad to speak aloud,
quiet
with more to say,
lonely
at the close of day,
exhausted
with no solace in sleep,
anxious
with only memories to keep
the pain
from replacing me.

— 9/28/19

# first night

Do you remember building our cabin, my love?
The dreaming, the planning, the search for land,
teasing out the design, rustic and log-sided,
everything on a budget,
doing all we could ourselves.
That first season in the woods,
clearing the lot, your asthma so daunting,
ten minutes hauling brush demanded an equal rest,
but you stuck there, weekend after weekend,
no prizefighter preparing for a bout
ever more determined, or training harder,
as we worked in the heat and the blackflies,
those goddamned blackflies,
every bit of disturbed vegetation
unleashing a cloud of angry, sentient, black pollen,
unerringly seeking our faces, mouths, eyes, ears,
your fetching beekeeper's helmet
and DNA scrambling doses of repellent a meager defense,
but by summer's end,
miraculously, counter-intuitively,
you could work the morning,
break for lunch,

then the afternoon, unstoppable,
your dream of health and perpetual motion realized,
the new lightweight champion.
On and on, hole dug, footings poured,
you and I alone in the woods, together,
laying up the foundation walls of our dream,
huge foam blocks, like giant styrofoam Lego,
the latest thing, trailblazers you and I.
The outer shell, pre-built, arriving on tractor-trailers,
walls, gables, log rafters effortlessly flown into place
by skilled hands behind a vintage, baby blue crane,
all in a steady autumn rain,
of course it had to rain, all week,
cold, wet, foggy, miserable,
sodden October leaves underfoot,
a slippery, kaleidoscopic carpet,
when finally, roof panels slung into place,
it was tight and secure, but hollow,
like an old tree seeking feathery tenants.
Another year of weekends, vacations,
as we framed and wired, plumbed and sheetrocked,
until, at last, that second December,
not quite finished, but close enough,
we rented a tiny, million-mile Toyota,

a little clown-car of a truck, lone orphan on the lot,
cab-over box on its tired back,
its once bright U-Haul-It decals
peeling and faded to near transparency.
We stuffed that little truck with furniture,
like a cubist aluminum holiday turkey,
and set out to spend our first night
in the cabin we built, together.
As we ventured north and climbed,
it began to snow, flurries at first,
but then, my God, how it snowed,
snow pounding out of the blackened sky,
a tantrum of snow,
petulantly hurling itself at the ground,
wind-whipped drifts piling up as we drove, ever slower,
praying we'd make it, allowing we might not, until,
after a barely controlled descent down our road,
the unloading, on snow-drunk feet.
Exhausted, we heaved the last snow-anointed
bric-a-brac inside,
only to realize we had forgotten something
in our quest to christen our snug, warm, sleepy getaway:
food.

Hollowed from our labors,
not a stick of gum between us,
we debated going hungry,
waiting for the morning and the plows,
but our grumbling stomachs staged an insurrection,
pushing us back out into the blizzard.
Our wheezing little wreck of a rental truck
with the questionable summer tires,
its ass-end empty now and
swinging gaily back and forth
like a fossil fueled pendulum,
light as goose down, a child's helium filled Tonka toy,
ready to surf into a ditch on a wind-propelled whim,
as we started up the road we had only just made it down,
engine redlined, screaming,
— *REEEEEEEEEEEEEEEEEEE!* —
tires spinning wildly, out of all proportion to our progress,
that poor little truck fighting like a wounded Marine
for each forward inch up the hill,
battling through the drifts and ruts,
setting itself against the tempest,
darting left, sliding right,
pelted with snowy fire from all sides,
with us laughing, giddy and hypoglycemic,

exhorting it, "You can do it! You can do it, Little Truck!"
and somehow it responded, cartoonishly, now animated,
anthropomorphized into life,
joining us in the struggle, aching to show us
just what it was made of,
how much heart a worn-out little truck
could muster when it mattered, and when,
beyond all probability, we reached the crest,
we didn't know who was more thrilled,
us or that brave and devoted little bald-tired truck,
as we fetched our groceries
and crawled back to our hideout,
dinner and breakfast now within reach.
Do you remember that, my love?
But of course, you don't,
because you've passed beyond remembrance,
beyond the reach of blackflies and asthma,
cabins and snowstorms,
even silly, fearless little stout-hearted trucks,
your hunger now forever sated,
my hunger now only for you,
this precious memory mine alone to preserve.
When I fail this life, and the task,
where will that memory go,

with countless others,
all as dear to me as my blood?
Perhaps it will live on
in some forgotten country junkyard,
where a foolish, faithful little truck rests,
rusting and abandoned,
dreaming of the time when it proved its mettle,
did what it didn't know it was capable of,
fueled by our dream,
driven by our love.

— 10/11/19

# catnip

Each morning,
every night,
first and last words,
vulgar bookends
replete with despair,
rage, and self-pity,
exhausted desperation
at waking to the futile day to come,
relenting the barren one just ended,
spent with steadfast companions,
loss and grief,
assiduous, unflagging,
nourished by the anguish,
the impossibility of resolution,
rushing the dawn,
delaying the night,
covetous of more time
with their bagatelle.

— 10/22/19

# the play is the thing

I'm not the only one who's ever lost,
just the only one who ever lost you,
far from alone in paying love's cost,
just one more assessed a fine not yet due.

The script of our lives wasn't ours to control,
and grace anoints barely a favored few,
but our past was my future, written in gold,
and grace was your gift as I earned more of you.

In the first act, I confess, my vow was a lie,
when we promised to love until one of us died,
as I struggle to accept the truth that you're gone,
my love is your legacy, and the show must go on.

The world was our stage, you and I joyous players,
then your God stormed the set as silent betrayer,
ending your life, dissolving our pact,
now forsaken onstage through life's final act.

All the world's plays reach an end, to be sure,
but in some corner of hell our script was redacted,
a love edited out that was written to endure,
this hopeless soliloquy the sentence enacted.

— 10/28/19

# i scream, I.

If I say I hate raspberry ice cream,
no one expects me to blow up a Baskin-Robbins®,
but if I say I hate my life without you,
I see the concern, read the worry,
always there, if only in subtext,
"Is he okay?
Is he going to hurt himself?"
But don't you see,
the harm is already done?
My death,
in the wake of yours,
would be a papercut —
sudden, stinging,
yet quickly reconciled.
Frost would understand;
the life we led together,
like two roads diverging,
rests with you now, underground,
while I travel, alone, down another path,
and that is making all the difference.

# i scream, II.

"Okay" is a separate matter,
a state, light-years distant,
on a planet identical to this one,
conditions hospitable to life,
just not mine, in the absence of yours,
only adding to my mortal ambiguity,
so I will say it plainly;
I fear dying,
still human at the core,
but not its consequence,
the distinction revealed in the difference.
Death, like visiting the pyramids,
has no analog in life,
but the duress of the journey
and the opportunity for regret along the way,
provides the surety that I won't
willingly embark on a trip
for which there is no need, because,
while I cannot be impelled to Egypt's tombs,
all roads, well-trodden and black,
will return us to the unrecallable void
from which we emerged,
no intervention required.

— 11/2/19

# 1 Corinthians 13:11*

When I was a child, atomic missiles hurtled noiselessly
through the firmament, aimed, as far as I knew, directly
at my school just down the street, the nearest desk
I could hide under and resist the urge to look at the
flash, which the man in the film said would damage
my eyes, and then where would I be, instantly
carbonized, but too blind to find my way to the
graveyard up the hill to mourn my lost innocence?

If missiles weren't enough, there were the gosh-darned
Communists, lurking everywhere, but I had no beef
with Communists, consumed as I was with more
immediate quandaries than the Red who might be
teaching my gym class as I unwittingly did pushups
for the Politburo. No, I struggled with meatier matters,
like why in the name of Gumby and Pokey did hotdog
rolls come in sixes when hotdogs came in eights?
My times-tables stunned brain couldn't parse the
number of packages of six buns, X, that might
eventually contain the number of hot dogs in packages of
eight, why?, as algebra still slouched beyond a
far-off horizon, but no matter, as I suspected my

mother couldn't be wheedled into such an
instinctively huge purchase.

Still, when my dad drove a Chevrolet with
fender-mounted jets that obviously provided
the propulsion — how could it be in an age of
jet-powered cars that I lived in a world with either
too many hot dogs or too few rolls? How, whooshing
along the highway at extra-sonic speeds, one eye
squinted and the other peering down my pointer
finger, tip turned devastating buzzsaw in my
imagination, scything down the trees lining the road
as we hurtled along, our shimmering wake littered
with fallen oaks and chestnuts, maples and elms — was
no one able to untie this gastronomic Gordian knot?

My childish understanding was revised as I learned
about internal combustion engines, got bored and
abandoned my buzzsaw finger, and became wise to the
tricks of marketers, the bun conundrum just a tactic
to get our moms to buy a second package. And the
missiles. There were no goddamned missiles shearing
the atmosphere in perpetual reentry, there were only
the bourbon-soaked, cigar-smoked, paranoid wargasms

of the impotent old men who ran the world,
secure in their own MADness, but suffering
the children with the threat of the Red Menace and
Strangelovian Armageddon, keeping us in line,
grooming us for the battlefields and canons
("Uncle Sam Needs YOU!") of their flaccid rage.

Soon enough grown, independent, educated and
married, secure in a well-ordered world of science
and medicine, where vaccines prevented disease,
germs could be conquered, viruses subdued,
and symptoms led to diagnoses and treatment,
only to have that world implode in a blinding flash,
as a Communist encephalopathy infiltrated
your immune system, allowing tiny intracranial
ballistic missiles to slip in undetected and detonate
in your brain, forming the lesions that ravaged
your perception, jamming the signals to your muscles,
leaving your sweet essence unharmed, but lashing us
to our seats at a beggar's banquet of suffering and rage,
where you, the guest of honor, and I, your helpless,
hopeful squire, dined on a daily smorgasbord of
speculation, tests, incompetence, misdiagnoses and
casual cruelty, consumed once again with

the childhood mismatch between rolls and dogs,
now symptoms and treatment.

We might as well have sought remedy from our
childhood icons Mr. Moose and Bunny Rabbit,
crouched under your hospital bed, eyes averted,
waiting for the promised fireball and gamma ray storm
for all the good the doctors at the world-famous
hospital did. In the end, and it was the end, no
diagnosis, no hope, and the only therapy that worked
as marketed was the fucking morphine, as we were sent
on our way, forced to say goodbye to each other and
our life together for the very last time, and I buried you
along with the childish faith that all problems have
solutions, and all of life doesn't end in a steady rain
of missiles and darkness, radiation and carbon.

— 11/10/19

* "When I was a child, I talked like
a child, I thought like a child, I
reasoned like a child. Now an adult,
I have no more use for childish ways."

# a thought experiment, with minor illustrations, as alternative to current theory

**In the Beginning**

We postulate that this
was the 'Big Bang':

(Everything)

Every..........thing

---

E V E R Y T H I N G

---

every object,
every force,
every law,
physics,

( et al, IN TOTO )
jammed in
the tiniest preatomic Tupperware,
all of time, the entire Universe,
(restrained.)

Then
)))) *offcamethelid* ((((
&:
Bang.

A while later,
Us.
Not a bad theory.

But what if —
(stay with me —
: here :
& flex your mind to this)
what if we have it wrong?

Ready? Here we go. (Humor me.)
***Initiate.***

Imagine yourself at the Big Bang, milliseconds after.
Now fast-forward.

No, *really* fast…
*Much, much, MUCH faster.*

*Eons, epochs, millennia,*
and so on and so on and nowwww…
slow down,  slow  down,  *s l o w  d o w n*
….. *and*
HARD STOP on my mark —
***3 - 2 - 1*** — *MARK!*

Well done.
Welcome back to Earth, around now.
The Atacama Desert.
Night.
Stiletto clear, no moon.
0100 hours.

Look around.
No.  No, no,
UP, look up
& around you.

Now speed it up a bit.

See the reeling, spinning, expanding universe. *Feel it.*

*Feel it* accelerating, hurling apart

to its future/destination:

**Entropy**

aka

**[Heat death]**

Heat death = all done.

Tank empty.

Out of gases.

Last gases for $10^{100 \text{ to the trillion trillion}}$ yearmiles.

No more stars,

no more galaxies, nebulae, black holes, light, mass,

waves, particles.

***Lots*** more nothing. All, now nothing.

I n f i n i t e nothing.

Utter **darkness**.

Utter, utter quiet. Library quiet to the $^{\text{nth power }+1}$,

a **thick** vacuum of . (Period, end of **everything**.)

Ab-so-lute paralyzed equilibrium,

cold, bitter cold, blackest bitter cold,

freezing subatomic soup.

Now what if (just a thought)
the issue isn't what came be***fore***
the Big Bang,
(thinking in ***t,*** time)

*but….*

What was on the ***"other side"*** of the ***singularity***
("behind it," thinking in **x-y-z** dimensions)
the moment before the lid came off?
And what if, just thinking aloud,
what was "behind" it was…
a wormhole?

A wormhole, you see,
not time, not gravity,
nor inconceivable quanta,
but:
a gateway.

Creo quia absurdum est,*
a singularity, not as pending event,
but rather

the terminus of a

wormhole.

And what if,
on the other "end?"

Of the wormhole?

A lab.
A
**GINORMOUS**,
god-scale sized,
deity-run, universe(al) lab —

*brimming* with experiments,
experiments with a CAPITAL **E**.
Deus mio, what Experiments!
Some still running:
gassy, noisy,
bellowing,
shiny, silent,

shimmering, exploding,
messy, reproducing
experiments.

Some completed.

Some **BIG,**

**HUGE**, even.

Some **tiny.**

And some failed.

And what if the singularity/wormhole
is sometimes and at once a singularity/wormhole *and...*
an interstellar cannula?

(You see it coming now, yes?
Sehr gut, mein Freund!)

And what if our "today"
(this day, all days past, every day yet to come)
is just what's happening
in our composting universe

if the Deity's Lab Assistant,
tasked to do some cleaning up,
slammed back the door to the wormhole,

with a **BIG BANG**

&

just threw out the trash?

— 11/12/19

**I believe because it is absurd*

# isolation as a trick of light and perspective: print and negative

Muted, sun-freckled library,
snug cocoon, near-spring afternoon,
hidden corner, denim-polished leather armchair,
arms-length radiator mumbles white noise.
Immersed, contented, in
caramelized, book-scented, vintage air,
transported, flying with giants,
untethered, married to the world,
alone.

Pair-bonded, life-partnered,
decades of deathless, star-brilliant love,
sudden grim illness,
finest self utterly gone,
no route across the divide,
denial, belief,
offering, prayer
by turns repudiated,
darkness settles into

cauterized consciousness,
exsanguinated heart,
culled from the world.
Alone.

— 11/16/19

# all is lost

*Future*

as empty as a rattlesnake's heart.

*Past*

as wistful as a teddy bear's dream.

*Now*

as pointless as a runner's false start.

*Reality*

as stable as a home built of steam.

*Dreams*

as hollow as a prisoner's ambition.

*Plans*

as futile as a diver's last breath.

*Hopes*

as likely as God's true contrition,

*Grief*

as complete as my love's tender death.

— 11/22/19

# applemath

Two apples,
take away one,
elementary reckoning,

the absent apple,
fate unaccounted,
forever beckoning,

presence defined
in the chiaroscuro
of absence,

solution replaced
by sorrow
for the subtracted,

the remainder
an afterthought now,
the equation redacted.

— 12/5/19

# seeking, never to find

My hopeless heart beats on, undaunted,
like a spirit unwilling to leave the house it haunted
after death and heartbreak bound it forever
to the home and hearth of its dearly lost lover.
I roam this place in fruitless search
of the words or the sermon, the healing or church,
that might release me from this echoing prison,
or at least lend voice to the logic or reason,
of the scourge or the god that would commit such blasphemy
as to wrest your presence, your life, away from me,
leaving me here in desperation so exquisite
that despite all the calls and the cards and the visits,
whether daylight or darkness, the incalculable distance
from my heart to yours is met with resistance
to the untenable thought that you're departed forever,
and no measure of yearning will bring us together,
but still my crippled heart insists, all evidence spurned,
it must beat on in hope of your gentle return.

— 10/6/19

# death as a life sentence

No guards, no walls,
no noisy mess hall;
no gates, no wires,
no riots, mattress fires.

Time's my own,
do as I please;
read, write,
watch the TV.

Food's no good,
have to make my own
in this prison that looks
just like our home.

Don't remember the trial,
just woke here one day;
no other inmates,
so not much to say.

Security's minimum,
leave if I choose,
truck in the yard
seems free to use.

Suppose I could run,
but end of each day
I wind up back here,
just locked away.

If I had a last wish,
probably not permitted,
I'd wish for you, here,
forever committed.

— 12/7/19

# ghost of funeral past

One year ago,
seated before the altar,
I mourned you at the inaugural
of the end of our life.

In that same hour today,
the sad ghost I am now
returned to the shrine
of that bitter anniversary

to find a baptism underway,
renovating the echo of your last rites.
From the last pew
I bore silent witness

to the rituals of a newborn life,
as I wept over the remains of ours.
I departed quietly,
a poltergeist with no role in that play,

unseen, unremarked, unrequited,
and made my solemn way to the graveyard,
the very last specter in your funeral procession,
the very first in hers.

— 12/14/19

# a year and a day

The cortege of time
stained black
by your indelible absence
appends a pivotal day,

a mythical inflection point,
threshold of resignation
to an expired fate
fraught with renewal,

but the wreckage lies unreconciled,
no different this day
from the prior or the next,
reclamation inconceivable,

plans and raw material
devoured in the charnel house fire,
essential tools dulled and de-tempered
past any remedy of sharpening.

Do not watch this space,
nothing coming soon;
there will be no grand reopening
under renewed management.

— 12/15/19

# pyre

When there was nothing left to donate to the flames,
I would have added my skin, eyes, hands,
had they been prescribed as your remedy,
reunited on the pyre with
my combustible rage and charcoaled heart,
my breath become cinder-flecked smoke,
roiling the night with a spiraling, enervated wind.

But the inferno would not be satiated
until the whole of you was consumed,
sacrificed without justification or cause,
leaving the sour stink of smoldering, tear-soaked ash,
and the fear that as the embers dim
I must lose you again, or lose myself,
the only salvage my incendiary, inflammable grief.

— 12/21/19

# wish fulfillment

I want
to look out the window and see you
ripping around the corner of our drive,
top down, silver hair flying,
zipping up the hill to the garage,
and know I'll be holding you moments from now.

I want
to enter our house
and hear you call out my name with delight,
happily welcoming me home
no matter whether I'd been gone
for an hour or a day.

I want
to look over and see you
gently asleep on your couch,
warmed beneath your angel blanket,
smiling, perfectly relaxed,
knowing, even while you dream,
nothing could trouble you while I am near.

I want
to stop crying,
to know you're safe,
protected as I would protect you,
to know your pain is gone
and you're content to wait,
as long as you must,
to call out my name one last time.

And because I can have
none of those things,
the last thing I want
is to stop wanting.

— 12/29/19

# Sherlock Holmes and the case of the missing spouse

"He lived at the corner, Watson, of Nightmare and Dream,
in a dreary old place of better days seen,
with his future a past that had already been
written, before we laid sight on that desolate scene."

"His life was a shambles, condemned to destruction,
knocked from its foundation by a fateful abduction,
his existence now become an abstract production,
all inferred through elementary deduction."

"There's her grave, so it follows there was a life,
he's her husband, so it follows she was his wife,
relatively young, so likely there was medical strife,
so many flowers, it seems he was gutted, as if by a knife."

"Frozen footprints in the snow,
obviously he kept himself near,
so many tracks, one surmises he held her quite dear,
without her his life surely felt beyond drear,
and any way forward was undoubtedly unclear."

"I believe if we proceed to excavate the scene
of the rubble that sits at Nightmare and Dream,
we'll find lying somewhere beneath the ashes and steam,
the remains of our man, below fallen beams."

"The solution may seem somewhat prosaic,
to succumb to something so vaguely archaic
as the notion that life's remaining mosaic
no longer beckoned, after a loss so cruel, yet so basic."

— 1/13/20

# left behind

When I lost my sister, I lost my inspiration.

When I lost my brother, I lost my hero.

When I lost my mother, I lost my example.

When I lost my father, I lost my model.

When I lost you, I lost my tether to this world,

my purpose,

my air.

— 1/17/20

# untying the not

No beginning to each day,
no air at your grave,
no end to the nights,
nor need to be brave.

No impression in your chair,
calls from people you knew,
no blanket on your couch,
nor being your beau.

No new pictures to take,
nor watering your flowers,
no more sunsets to gift you,
nor soft, contented hours.

No touch at the end of my reach,
calling out your name,
loving to make you laugh,
no end to loss or pain.

No anniversaries to measure,
nor watching as you sleep,
no more sighs in the night,
nor happy secrets to keep.

No lying next to me,
silly jokes, pet names,
no frigid feet against my leg,
no more playing our games.

No music from your piano,
gifts to give or receive,
no rattle at the door,
no "Hurry back!" when I leave.

No more now, just forever,
nor walks around our land,
no more top-down adventures,
nor simply holding your hand.

No more "Remember when's…?"
no way to live or to be,
No "Hi, Honey!," from the top of the stairs,
no pride, without you to see.

No more chattering away,
no one to share getting old,
no one here to comfort,
no one to have and to hold.

No sitting together at dinner,
haircuts to critique,
no one to hold me as I die,
no New Year's Eve, fast asleep.

No way back, nor home,
no someone to adore.
At the last, no me and you;
never less, and now no more.

— 1/18/20

# guilty as charged

As treatment failed
and symptoms worsened,
a decision was compelled
to mediate your suffering.

In our conscripted trinity
of doctor, patient and spouse,
we were mercy bound to discuss
the end.

Though we knew
what was going to happen,
what was happening,
you were,
*(and how could you not have been,*
*who would not have been?)*
reluctant.

It fell to me, then,
your protector and fiercest guardian,
the one sworn never to harm you,
to become your executioner.

Terrified, desperately alone,
I assented to a plan
to ease your approaching death,
prescribing an end to the life
I would have ended my own to preserve.

There are
no meetings or minutes,
no roll calls or reunions,
of this guild I was loathe to join,
this fractured confederacy of Hobson's ghosts,

forever damned for choosing the unthinkable,
unforgivable, impossible,
changing everything but the outcome,
each of us lost to the other,
and the world.

— 1/29/20

# forever is a day

Life in the vacuum
born of your absence
requires, moment
by airless moment,
cautiously navigating
the minefield
of the day ahead,
a day that will last
precisely as long
as the balance of my life.

— 2/8/20

# fundamental

Slow without fast
place with no holder
first without last
old but no older

Sonnet with no heart
care without caring
end with no start
fool with no errand

Right with no left
gravity without mass
weight with no heft
future without past

Love with no lover
curse with no hex
battlefield without cover
now with no next

Above without below
sky with no air
light wanting shadow
a wound with no care

Hunger with no ease
profanity without heresy
forest with no trees
pleas but no mercy

Point with no line
universe without space
clock out of time
steps without pace

Tears without end
a way with no through
curve with no bend
my life without you

— 2/9/20

# holding pattern

Where to put this death,
darkness that
infiltrates every space,
warps thought,
frustrates action,
rejects solace?

Radioactive with pain,
it counters sleep,
remands pleasure,
observes no boundaries.

It dictates the chemistry
that comprehends it,
commands tears,
nourishes guilt,
inflames rage.

How to contain the monster
when the monster is
omnipresent,
cancerous,
metastasized,
and will not be tempered?

— 2/9/20

# past tense

Was, were, used to be
never described us,
had no meaning in our life,
a widescreen, single-take movie,
seamless years of endless now,
now ended,
rendering it unbearable
to think of you — now —
to speak of you — now —
in the past tense,
what we knew as our life
archived in memory,
a bruised portfolio of
pale watercolor facsimiles
bound together by
what was ours,
what we were,
what we used to be.

— 2/16/20

# pale by comparison

The texture of the darkness
deified by your absence.

The cant of a world
lacking your presence for balance.

Color on blank canvas,
no hand to grace the brush.

The silence of our home,
no voice to dispel the hush.

Living displaced by death,
words and language fail.

All of time revealed in spectral light,
a dreary cache of pale.

— 2/29/20

# hummingbird

Life passed in a blur
with the rush of a hummingbird's wings,
decades transited with implausible speed,
pausing here and there,
mid-air,
for the briefest moment,
for us to appreciate,
together,
hovering, beautiful, perfect,
then gone,
so fast it's hard to say
how it ever reached this sad place,
where it goes from here,
or how it ends,
easier remembered than seen.

— 2/29/20

# satisfaction

I want revenge.
I want to fight for you,
physically battle,
destroy your attacker with my fists,
feet, teeth, screams,
bone, muscle, sinew,
fight to retrieve you
from the fucking faceless, nameless,
relentless miscreation
that stole you from me,
exposed me as an impotent fool,
believing for so many years that
I was your protector,
that I could defend you,
ready to forfeit my life for you without regret,
only to be cuckolded by an unseen, unknown scourge,
no flesh and blood villain to repel,
only medical inexperience, incompetence
and indifference,
with me, your hapless knight errant,
carrying you from one disappointment to the next,
hopelessly trying to keep the doctors from looking away

or killing you with their misdiagnoses and mistakes,
unable in the end to extract even a goddamned apology,
much less a pound of flesh or pint of blood.

I want a time machine.
I want to go back and see
with these bleeding, tear-ravaged eyes,
the signs I missed,
the too subtle clues that you were being
meticulously assaulted
by whatever hell-spawned pestilence was dining on you,
then rage at your physicians to open their eyes,
try harder, not write you off,
because if we had started earlier
maybe there would have been time to name it,
slow it, halt it, destroy it,
or at the least, keep it from killing you,
and if I fail in that mission and
I must die inside, again, as I watch you die again,
I would return a thousand more times,
ten thousand,

and even at the end, if I still fail you,
I will have lived your death over and over
until I, at least, got that right.

I want to fistfight your God.
I want to throw your life in his face,
his devoted child, martyred to the anaerobic wolf that
savaged your body and gnawed at your mind,
and demand his reason for this obscene injustice.
I want to charge at, hurl myself at him,
stain his robes with my blood, my sweat, my guts,
in the vainglorious hope
that fighting him to my own inevitable obliteration
exposes his wasted omnipotence,
makes him see that his experiment has failed
and it's time to confess *his* sins
and fix it,
or simply clean house,
either way, bestowing me the satisfaction
of no longer living in his hollow, hallowed nightmare.

— 2/29/20

# relativity

Twelve-foot poles in ten-foot barns,
fantastic trains
flashing through the universe
at the speed of light,
headlights illuminating the stars,
too much for my undergraduate brain,
now comprehensible
as you continue to fly away from me
at the speed of life.

The decades we reveled in
now measure a day,
no more than two,
while each day
alone on this deserted platform,
imagining your light-speed locomotive
as it transits forever,
is decades long.

— 3/5/20

# peace in another time

House so quiet you can hear a heart ache,
light so brittle
you can watch each day break.

Life slouches on, granted no other choice,
silence unbroken,
as there's no other voice.

The heart lacks the means to banish the want,
as memory persists
like a ghost in its haunt.

Life, like sin, can be unforgivable,
remaining days spent
learning to live the unlivable.

— 3/10/20

# portrait of a picture

The photo is of a woman,
nestled against a post
on the edge of a log-cabin porch,
smiling up at the man she loves.

Vermont autumn-sun backlight,
all the colors of the world they shared,
breathes golden fire into her auburn bob.

Luminous shadow caresses her face,
too shallow to conceal her beauty,
her joy, the way she loved,
a radiance no shade could eclipse.

The woman had many gifts,
but a special one for painting,
and the man asked her to render
the picture as a self-portrait.

Neither dreamed that this canvas
would be the only one
she would ever paint of herself
or that it would later grace an easel

in an old, incense-smoked church,
beside an urn,
the woman become illustrator
for her own funeral mass.

The shadows are everywhere now,
plentiful and deep,
golden light consumed
by insatiable twilight,

as the man sits quietly, lost,
and gazes up at the portrait
painted from the picture of the woman in love,
smiling down at the man she loved.

— 3/14/20

# wasted

Picture
the fastest sprinter in the world
never rising from their chair,

a brilliant diagnostician
never providing care,

the foremost mountaineer
spending their life at sea,

a visionary builder
living as lessee,

the singular, shining diva
who never deigns to sing,

the monstrous gift of omnipotence,
and never amending a thing.

Who would not ask why?
And why would you not answer?

— 3/17/20

# end of day

The light in life is gone,
leaving nothing left to lose,

no choices left worth making,
and none I'd wish to choose,

no price left to pay,
no means to satisfy the debt,

no reason left to stay,
but the time's not here,
not yet.

— 3/23/20

# stars

One by one,
the stars burn out,
never revealing
what they're all about.

They glimmer, they shine,
they loiter in the sky,
born into fire,
destined to die.

One day, it is said,
the stars will be gone,
the universe turned black,
neither right nor wrong.

But until perfect dark
murmurs final goodbye,
you and the stars
will grace the night sky.

— 3/29/20

# logic of the non sequitur

Revenge is a dish, like albatross,
best offered and served with tea.
Hate's the emotion, like applesauce,
sweeter than it has right to be.

Sadness is like a marriage,
a way of never saying goodbye.
Tears anoint your face with courage,
but argue it's time to cry.

Anxiety, a frosted blight,
serves none but those it frees.
Fear creeps in on godless nights
when dreams provide no ease.

Living makes no sense to the dead,
who have no tears to dry.
Dying, like a dog seeking its bed,
circles before it lies.

— 4/5/20

# the first 101 things

Your hum of delight when I swaddled you in hot laundry,
fresh from the dryer.
Your smoky voice,
and easy, delighted, and delightful laugh.

The radiant smile that lit up your face
when you looked at me,
your persistence in getting my attention early on,
and your never ridiculing my fear of snakes.

Your unwavering support for life's underdogs,
love of any and every baby animal,
your wonderful malapropisms,
which I never let you forget,
and your ability to laugh at yourself — and me.

Your charity,
your quiet, personal faith,
and your easy acceptance of my lack of same.
The way you dealt with adversity
and never, ever pitied yourself.

That you knew, months before you died, before the
doctors would even say it, that you were dying, and never
once did you ask, "Why?" much less "Why me?"
That you remained the same person, cheerful and
content throughout your trial, making friends in every
encounter with the people trying to save you.
That at the end you so loved your roommate that you
chose not to come home to die, because it would have
been cruel to your new friend to leave her.

The way you anthropomorphized your stuffed animals and
loved your VW convertible, the only car you ever
thought of as being more than
a toaster with wheels, and oddly,
the way it adopted a personality remarkably like yours,
delighted with the attention she would receive when the
two of you were out and about, with her top more likely
to be down than up in any kind of weather except rain.

Never letting your health get in the way of anything
you wanted to do,
and your, "Is that all you got?!" attitude towards
life's vicissitudes.
Your self-effacing modesty about

your many accomplishments,
your empathy for your incarcerated clients,
and your forbearance of my pessimism.

Your love of chocolate
and your discipline in not eating too much chocolate.
The way your eyes shone when you looked at me,
your industriousness,
your feminism, not as artifice, but simply as part
of who you were.

That you were more intelligent than me, but never
agreed with that simple fact.
That you never tired of playing our lover's games,
and there was no question in my heart
that you loved me,
and none in yours that I loved you.

That when I came home to our apartment one night
and said, "I think we should build a house,"
you simply said, "Okay,"
and spent the next two years of weekends tramping
across, up, down and over every godforsaken piece
of swampland and mountain-goat habitat

in the county with me,
looking for the right parcel of land,
and when we finally found it, we made an offer
the same day,
and lived there the rest of your life.

That we agreed instantly on a builder,
then on one of his plans,
and when he was suspicious because we made decisions
too quickly and agreed with each other so easily, afraid
we'd start making changes after the build was underway,
you said, "No we won't."
And we didn't.

That you happily spent weekends with me cleaning up
the jobsite, back-priming clapboards, and doing the
1,001 other tedious things we did to save money
and make the house ours,
and when it was done, you moved everything but our
furniture into it from the back of your little Honda,
load after load, while I was at work,
then secretly arranged for our furniture to be moved
so I wouldn't have to do it.

That when life didn't meet your expectations,
you simply, genuinely,
lowered your expectations.
That at a time long before the feminist movement,
when jobs appeared in the classifieds as Jobs for Men
and Jobs for Women, you would routinely
apply to any job that interested you, regardless,
and knowing they used only male waiters at the time,
you once applied to Anthony's Pier 4,
just to make them turn you down.

That among your employment adventures, you were
once a frozen turkey broker
and worked at a Pewter Pot Muffin House in Boston,
where two muffins and a coffee were $.75, inevitably
resulting in a quarter tip, and because people loved you,
you made a very good living $.25 at a time.

That you got the job that led to us meeting and marrying
when the hiring manager asked if you slept with the boss
and you told him, "You'll have to hire me to find out."
So he did.
And you didn't.

That you never once boasted about being a
US Women's National Judo Champion,
and when I proposed climbing Mt. Monadnock for our
first official date, not knowing you had asthma and a
detached ACL from your judo career, and even though
your knee gave out and you fell down the last few stairs
of my apartment on our way out the door, you insisted
you were fine, so we went and climbed a mountain
because you had already decided you were going
to marry me and didn't want to let anything get
in the way of that plan —
and we never parted from that day forward.

That you took up skiing because I was a skier,
and loved it,
so you took lessons and practiced until you were an
expert long before I was,
and when you decided we should build a ski cabin,
you were right there beside me in the woods that
first summer, cutting and hauling brush.

That for years you thought the photographer
who stalked Jackie Kennedy was
an Italian gentleman named Papa Razzi,

and when a friend told you you'd love law school, having
never before even considered it, that same day you drove
to WNE Law School, checked it out, signed up, and
became a lawyer just a few years later.

That you studied for the bar exam listening to practice
tapes in your car while driving to and from Stratton on
weekdays so you could get in a few hours skiing and then
race home before I got back from work,
and I never knew that until you told me years later,
because you didn't want me to feel bad that
you were skiing while I was working,
and you genuinely thought the bar exam was easy,
passing it on your first try.

Your obsession with your haircuts
and fretting about each new one,
without a shred of vanity,
just wanting it to be right,
and even though I was the one you turned to, and
I thought they always looked wonderful,
I'm not sure you believed me even once, ever.

That you made friends more easily
than anyone I ever met,
always drawn to people who really needed friends,
and were so innocent that you were always disappointed
when a potential male friend would mistake
your kindness for flirting.

That you rode a yellow Vespa scooter to and from
Cathedral High School long before that would have been
considered acceptable, especially at Cathedral, and once
set out for a beach ninety miles from home, with a
girlfriend riding backward behind you on your tiny,
smoky scooter, where, for lack of funds, the two of you
slept on the beach and were nearly consumed by the
mosquitoes and beach flies you hadn't anticipated, but
you made it there and back without life-changing
incident, though not without being stopped by a
policeman, who was so flabbergasted at what the two
of you were doing, he made your friend turn around,
told you to be careful, and let you go on your way.

That in the nearly forty years I knew you,
though you were stopped multiple times,
you never once got a ticket,

because you were honest and guileless,
so much so that you asked an officer who stopped you
for speeding one day to please hurry and write you
a ticket because you just had to get to Pittsfield
to see your little sister —
and you still didn't get a ticket — or slow down
after you were out of sight.

That you demurred at my suggestion
that you write an autobiography,
despite your compelling life story and
all the things you overcame,
because you didn't want the attention,
and that despite every obstacle life and circumstance
ever put in your way, you were the most hopelessly,
relentlessly, determinedly optimistic person
I've ever met.

That you arranged our wedding in less than an hour
with three phone calls,
and you thought it was a hoot to elope to Florida
and be married by a female JP
in the Sleepy's Hollow garden behind the
Disney Inn at 7:30 in the morning,

where I had to ask the groundskeeper
to shut his mower off for fifteen minutes
(which he was happy to do)
so we could hear ourselves exchange our vows.

That on the only official vacation we ever took,
we were both so bored by Thursday that we came home
and went to work repairing the apartment house
we lived in and owned at the time, happy as the clams
we left behind in Cape Cod Bay.
That you never questioned my devotion to my family,
as much as they sometimes irritated you.
That you ate an alarmingly healthy diet,
not because it was the right thing to do,
but because you loved all the healthy foods.
That your two favorite movies were
"Starman" and "Enemy Mine,"
one for its hopeless romance,
the other for the baby Drak.

Maybe it was the judo training
(though I think it was just you),
but I can't recall ever seeing you intimidated by anyone,
your fierceness so quiet, so blisteringly logical, that it

would sneak up on people,
and your prodigious memory,
to which I often fell victim.

Your not wanting to own anything, even insisting that
once we bought something,
like our sofa, it was mine, not yours.
That your love of looking at the real estate ads
each week in no way affected your love of our home
and our place in the world.

That twenty years later you still delighted in imitating
the speech patterns of the much, and as far as you were
concerned, unjustly maligned Jar Jar Binks,
who you loved for his innocence and lack of guile.
That you never noticed you shared those qualities
with Jar Jar Binks.
That you never made an issue of my abhorrence
for backtracking
once we were headed somewhere.
That when I mentioned getting a recumbent bike,
you instantly wanted one, too,
loved it, and we rode together at every opportunity.
The ease with which you learned to paint,

and the beautiful portraits you produced
and happily gifted to people
just for the joy it gave you.
That when a developer wanted to build a disastrously
polluting industrial operation on land across the road
from our home, in a public meeting
you asked him what his mother thought of the plan,
and when he responded, "She thinks I'm crazy,"
you told him he should listen to his mother.
Not to mention your serene and unwavering confidence
right from the start, despite my panic,
that he wouldn't succeed,
and your modesty when it turned out you were right.

The immense pleasure you derived from having
tea with friends
and planting flowers in your gardens with your
"adopted sister"
until you couldn't any longer.
Your love of the ocean.
That you never stopped being curious or learning.
That you loved going to the movies or
watching them at home,
and in all of our years, even though you never asked

for the remote,
you drew the line at endless shows about building cars
and gold mining.
Your certainty that I would always change the channel
if you asked me to.

That your rule for buying clothes was that
we both had to like them,
and when you decided to let your hair go naturally silver,
you never looked back.
That you made me a better person than I ever could have
been on my own,
or with anyone other than you,
and you were even more beautiful on the day you died
than on the day we met.

— 4/10/20

# stars, too

The stars lie,
not as they appear,
hung in night's sky,

seen through tears,
interstellar collage
of billions of years,

many dead, the rest dying,
postmortem beauty
more horrifying

than whatever awaits
far side of a grave,
nothing left to give,
no one left to save.

— 4/11/20

# plurals

A trepidation of hopes
desiccation of dreams
sandstorm of plans
concussion of schemes

A disgrace of regrets
cesspool of fears
anguish of memories
upheaval of tears

An exequy of firsts
finity of lasts
cataract of futures
obsequy of pasts

— 4/11/20

# for my dad, James

A sturdy, powerful man from stubborn, Scottish stock,
he became the youngest of eight minus one when his
baby brother was taken by measles and pneumonia,
carried away by a nurse from their home into the dark,
promised salvation of a hospital, back when such things
happened, next seen at his wake and funeral.
Like 18-month-old Robert, he never recovered,
mourning the loss of his baby brother for eighty-seven
years, a man who never cried, the Depression having
stolen his tears, but always delivered to watery eyes
and quavering voice by the memory.

Now the runt, he bore the slings and arrows of his older
siblings, and his namesake father's incipient alcoholism,
coming in waves like the tide, barely resisted
until a cohort would inevitably say, "C'mon, Jim,
be a sport! Just one," and just as there's never one drop
of rain in a flood, there was never just one drink, and
Angry Jim would arrive in a torrent of Scotch whiskey.
There was sometimes no money for food, but there was
always money to feed the monster, so evening meals were
sometimes a meager pot of oatmeal, divided ten ways.

He loved and admired his hapless, hopeless father,
as a child does, but resolved never to become the
abusive drunk he could be, so for his entire life he
avoided alcohol, even during the war when his barracks
buddies, their nascent manhood threatened by his
teetotaling, determined to get him drunk, even if they
had to hold him and pour it down his throat.
Never violent, another trait of his father he abjured,
he stated simply that he wouldn't fight them, but he
would kill the first one of them he laid hands on when
they inevitably had to let loose, and something about
the sturdy boy from Massachusetts with iron hands
nearly twice the size of most caused them to let loose
their plan, grumbling that he was no sport,
so where was the fun in it anyway?

Though he had been ineligible for the draft due to a
medical issue, he insisted to the man he knew on the
draft board that he be allowed to join the fight, much
to the chagrin and anger of his young wife, but he had
to go because it was right, and was conscripted by his
connection to the Air Corps for his mechanical abilities,
where he trained as a flight mechanic, spending the war
preparing bombers just off the production line for battle

and repairing the battered ones that had managed to
limp home, doing his part to assure a steady supply of
whistling death to the Axis, and leaving behind much of
his hearing because no one thought to supply earmuffs to
the men surrounded by thundering pistons every day.

Once returned from war, life got back on track,
back to his job, held for him while he was away,
at a time when such things happened, his boss having
made up the difference in his civilian and military pay
for the years he was away, discreetly delivered
to his young wife each week. Two children arrived,
a boy and a girl, then nearly ten years after the first,
a surprising late-in-life lad, ill-conception
of a New Year's Eve, just when things had settled down
and the worst of child-rearing was behind them.
So it was to be three, then. That one would later write.

A mid-century life, hard won and poorly paid, loyal to
his employer for nearly fifty years, because loyalty was
honorable, and certainty was prized over opportunity by
the boy, now the man, with the uncertain upbringing.
Always near-poor, his new family was near-lower middle
class, getting by on hand-me-downs and ingenuity, as

James and his wife made do, grew vegetables, chickens
and pigs, and he supplemented their income with
side-gigs before there were any, plumbing and wiring,
upholstery and tiling, later auctions and flea markets
after his knees and leg veins signaled surrender.

One-by-one, all nursing childhood wounds, his siblings
vanished or died. Then came the first bypass,
ten years later the second, then the triple-A repair,
the accumulated time spent on heart-lung machines
bestowing a manageable case of pump-head and possibly
his later dementia. The crushing blows, the ones that
couldn't be recovered from, truly began to fall as
their daughter succumbed to leukemia at forty-six,
then first-son to a previously undiagnosed
genetic heart defect at sixty-one,
a lifetime of service to country and company
apparently not sufficient dues paid to ensure death
in the natural order.

His life of duty and service now consigned to caring for
his wife; they survived as a two-card house of cards, each
leaning on the other for the support they needed, with
trailing-son managing much of their lives, comforting

them with his frequent presence, at times much
to the chagrin of his own wife. Then James's wife
was lost to a fall in the home, him sitting by her bed
in the ICU, gently holding her frail hand
in his giant ones, believing she was getting better
as she rested in her coma and calmly melted away.

Then there were just two in this nuclear family of
the atomic age, plus a soon-to-be beloved caretaker,
nephew's wife, appearing as if by magic just when the
need was greatest, stepping in for his Air Corps PT
instructor, insisting on twice daily walks, loving care,
and proper nutrition, carrying this wounded soldier
for nearly four years, until consecutive nights spent
on the floor after slipping from his bed triggered
a cascade of changes in muscle and blood, requiring
a hospital, then a planned-to-be-brief nursing home stay,
ostensibly to recover.

He had often vowed in later years that he wouldn't last
long in a nursing home, he'd see to it, and always a man
of his word, he did, seething at having this dignity-free
sentence poured down his throat, so he set about killing
the first man he could lay hands on, this time himself.

Drinking little, eating less, counting down, aided and
abetted by the blood goblin myoglobin, less than ninety
days erased ninety-six years, his discomfort eased
in his final hours by the morphine he feared was being
used to poison him, but still wasn't quite enough
to prevent the pained grimace that crossed his face,
while he slept, as his heart stopped.

— 4/15/20

# life of the lightkeeper

I was a sailor once,
standing to the east with you
through years of reverence
over sapphire seas.

I'm a lightkeeper now,
in my glowering tower,
warning all to steer away,
nothing good awaits you here,

my shores littered
with shipwrecked souls
tending their own beacons,
consecrating uncharted waters.

I would tell you,
had I the heart,
every voyage comes to naught,
ceded from the start.

— 4/18/20

# rejection slip

I live in a novel
that lacks happy ending,
readers anxious to know
if I'll break before bending.

Will my end be dramatic,
battered past recognition,
or a struggle to dementia's gates,
sentenced to perdition?

Will it be a best seller
in every airport in hell,
or be remaindered in heaven,
after failing to sell?

To the critic's dismay
there will be no reviews,
the only opinion I need,
a reaction from you.

So I'll read it aloud,
alone, at your grave,
then let you choose my fate —
shall I perish or be saved?

— 4/17/20

# colors of late

Mind the color of fog,
thoughts a darker gray

sullen sun, muted in pewter sky,
clouds a shade of clay

nights as black as a miner's lungs,
the moon begun to rust

yellowed stars, dulled and wan,
grant wishes turned to dust

heart of cyanotic blue,
eyes a bloodshot red,

tarnished life, darkened and dull,
lights the orbit from here to dead.

— 4/14/20

# cursory rhyme

April showahs bring May chowdahs,
a stich in mine saves time,
when people ask me how I'm doing,
I often just say, "Fine."

But when Jack and Masie went upsy-daisy
to pail a fetch of pollen,
they lost their crown when all fell down,
and saw how far they'd fallen.

When all the king's horses and all the king's ducks
tried to set them right,
all woozy were the borograves,
and mimzy was their plight,

so they went to the old woman who lived in a boot,
cobbling her cures as she cries,
who said, "My dear, dear horses, and dearer ducks,"
(now eating their Christmas flies)

"Paddy Cake, the baker's man,
baked a torte of blackbirds, and Pharaoh freed the slaves,
but this little piggy goes to the graveyard at noon,
because only Jesus saves."

— 4/26/20

# who goes there?

I like my apples all pests aside.
I tan best in the dark and on the inside.

Deep in a dream, that's when I eat.
I prefer hearts of lettuce that don't skip a beat.

If it must be done now, it can wait until later,
and what's really the point of a reticent creator?

My favorite pet? The Ring-tailed Manatee.
You may think I'm blind, but then, don't you see?

Einstein has said, "Space is all curvy,
and full of black holes," which just makes me worry,

about holes in my Swiss, none black, so it seems,
where I live for the whipped, but not for the cream.

There's no reason in this rhyme,
in this rhyme without reason.
Some call that faith. I call that treason.

So if my point's been obscured by what's just been read,
then perhaps only one of us
would be better off dead.

— 5/14/20

# numerology

It is May 12, 2020, the 132nd day of the year and
the date the Donner Party departed
Missouri for California in 1846.
The sum of all the 2-digit numbers you can compose
from 1, 3 and 2 equals 132.

Had she not died at 46, my sister would have been
71 years old today,
the US Office of Personnel Management form number
for requesting a leave of absence,
and the last known pair of Brown Numbers[1].
After her leukemia diagnosis, just after Thanksgiving,
she lived 6 months.

It has been 515 days since you died.
515 is the HTTP status code for
an Internal Server Error,
and the sum of nine consecutive primes[2].

After your final bout of sepsis,
and under attack by a neurological disorder,
never identified,
you also lived 6 months.
Six is the smallest perfect number[3].

If I live to my actuarial life expectancy,
I have 5,250 days left, including today.
In California, a 5250 hold permits an individual to be
involuntarily confined in a locked psychiatric hospital.

My brother has been dead 146 months.
Shakespeare's Sonnet 146 is an appeal
to inner virtue over vanity
and ends with the words,
"And Death once dead, there's no more dying then."
146 is an untouchable number[4].

My mother passed away 94 months ago.
94 is the proton number of plutonium,
named after Pluto, when it was still a planet.
I lived at 94 Meridian St.,
where my mother suffered her fatal fall at ninety-six,
my entire childhood.
Her death has no half-life.

My father, a generous and gentle man,
has been deceased for 55 months,
the sum of the numbers 1 through 10
and the atomic number of cesium,
the softest element. He, too, died at ninety-six.

As of May 12, 2020, I have wept for you,
for me,
for us,
more than 1,000 times.
One-thousand is a natural number[5].

— 5/12/20

[1]*Brown numbers are pairs (m,n) of integers satisfying the condition of Brocard's problem. Brocard's problem asks to find the values of n for which n! + 1 is a square number,* $m^2$*, where n! is the factorial. The only known solutions are n = 4, 5, or 7. Pairs of these numbers (m,n) are called Brown numbers. There are only three pairs of Brown Numbers.*

[2]*A prime number (or a prime) is a natural number greater than 1 that is not a product of two smaller natural numbers.*

[3]*A perfect number is a positive integer that is equal to the sum of its positive divisors, excluding the number itself.*

[4]*An untouchable number is a positive integer that cannot be expressed as the sum of all the proper divisors of any positive integer (including the untouchable number itself).*

[5]*In mathematics, natural numbers are those used for counting, as in "There are three coins on the table," and ordering, as in "This is the second largest city in the country."*

# paradise lost

More why's than answers,
fewer treatments than cancers,
less frost than blight,
more fear than fright.

More loneliness than visits,
fewer hours than minutes,
more pain than heart,
more parted than apart.

Fewer cures than maladies,
more hell than paradise,
less time than planned,
more sentence than remand.

More pain than pills,
fewer cures than ills,
more scythe than knife,
more death, less life.

— 5/21/20

# faux

This isn't living.
This is some copy of a fax
of a fax of a copy,
blurred bytes blended
into a message-redacted,
typographic Rorschach.

This isn't living.
This is some brundlefly'd
coadunation of life, death, and a virus,
genetically fused, incurable.

This isn't living.
This is some song-ending,
snapped-strings scream of
*broken-glass-scraping-rusted-barbed-wire*
chord.

This isn't living.
This is some ad infinitum telenovela,
Möbius-stripped memories
ending and beginning
where they initiate and terminate.

This isn't living.
This is some
bloodless, protracted snuff film,
victim confined in a windowless, doorless room
where the padded walls whisper,
*"How long?...How long?...How long?"*

This isn't living.
This is
*steel-wool-nerve-scrubbing-pain*
in thought and memory,
boneless cancer taken hold in DNA,
narcotically immune,
implacable, ineradicable.

This isn't living.
This is a sharp needle-stick
of anthropomorphic Novocain,
quelling joy, benumbing happiness,
blunting cognition.

This isn't living.
This is what remains of our life.

— 5/28/20

# the carousel by the beach

The little girl, barely a toddler,
is drawn by the pulsing, colored lights
and oddly clanging music
emanating from the structure.
She knows light and music, but the shifting hues
and spellbinding notes tugging at her now,
carried aloft on the magic carpet of a summer's twilight,
are new in her experience,
reeling her in, a sweet little sunfish,
with no more power to resist their siren call
than an apple resists gravity.

Though the source is unfamiliar,
she feels no fear,
the magnetic pull so intense
no caution could arrest her accelerating,
top-heavy, forward momentum.

Her lengthening shadow,
a ghostly ebony tether,
no longer quite reaches back
to her trailing parents.
She simply relies that they're there,
but this isn't the time to check,
instinctively worried that turning away,
even for a moment,
might interrupt this alluring spell.

She wobbles into the pavilion,
all tight curls and baby fat,
and is stunned into a sudden stop —
gob-smacked (if she knew what that was)
by the giant, round extravagance before her,
her first carousel,
a magnificent, antique example of the species,
though she has no name for it.

There's simply too much for her to take in,
her stillness absolute,
adrenaline and endorphins flooding her brain,
a chemical tsunami of joy she's felt before,
but never like this.

This is — this is — BETTER!,
*betterthanicecream,*
*betterthanswings,*
*betterthanmyfavoritestory,*
*betterthanmyprincessdress!*
Perhaps it really isn't better than all those things,
but at this perfect, twilit moment,
it just — it just —
IS,
and she wouldn't trade whatever this is for any of them.

She hasn't the words to describe this —
this — this — *thing* from a magic lamp,
or the Tooth Fairy or Santa,
or all of them together along with the Easter Bunny,
this wheezing, rotating,
up-and-downing, glittering, flashing,
noisy, kaleidoscopic cacophony.

Every cartoon she's ever seen,
every storybook ever passed before her eyes,
whips through her tiny cerebrum,
as she frantically seeks some basis of comparison,
some understanding of

WHAT'S HAPPENING HERE??!!
but all of her limited references
pale before this wonder,
surely the most glorious thing in
ANYWHERE!

She has pieces of it.
She knows horseys.
She understands motion,
the up and down, round and round part;
the colored, flashing lights are Christmas familiar;
and of course, she's heard music,
but never in all her hours has she experienced them
together in this crackling, pulsing, electrified exhibition
dancing before her in a huffing, spinning, creaking,
singing, reeling, vibrant psychedelic mirage.

But just as she's watched her mother
turn some wobbly eggs and milk and silky white powder
into the edible, wearable wonder that is
BIRFDAY CAKE AND FROSTIN',
this, too,
this gyrating, loud, kinetic, frantic contraption
has assembled a few simple things she knows

into a visual confection that she never could have imagined,
even in her most fantastic, satisfied, technicolor dreams.

As her miniature being pledges itself
to the wondrousness before her,
her tiny fists clench at her sides.
Her arms begin to shake,
though she doesn't know it, doesn't feel it,
and start to levitate, out of her awareness,
commanded now by this thing before her,
rising inexorably into the air,
her pudgy elbows bent, her little fists
now fairly vibrating back and forth before her face,
her mouth agape in a perfect 'O',
eyes stretched open as wide as they'll go,
the only physical expressions she has
in her growing repertoire
to express how very, very much
she is so HAPPY to be
RIGHT HERE! NOW!
her cerebellum offering up the only physical tributes
her unbalanced little body can perform
while remaining upright,
inadequate though they may be
to praise the stupendousness she is seeing.

She's consumed by an indescribable feeling,
linked forever now with this giant
TOY!
of mountainous proportions,
a feeling she'll know only this once in her entire life,
because you can only encounter
your very, very first carousel once,
and move from innately believing you have
some understanding of what's possible in your world
into a realm where, now, apparently,
EVERYTHING!
is possible.
This is HERS! She OWNS it!

In a few moments
her daddy will scoop her into his arms,
whirl her into the air as
her little owl's head swivels about,
locked on the TOY,
and through their little girl,
he and her mother may experience again
perhaps a thousandth, a ten-thousandth,
of a wonder they once felt themselves,
but only that much,

for if permitted full recall of such discoveries,
their original impact,
we'd spend our lives in despair at the routine
they become.

When the moment has passed for them,
not grasping that time has ceased altogether
for their little girl,
and she would happily remain
RIGHT HERE, SPENDED
in this place for the rest of her endless life,
(if she knew what suspended meant)
they'll add to her understanding
in that sing-song voice parents use to talk
to their children,
slowing on the words they expect her
to have trouble with,
as if that somehow helps.
"Look at that! *(As if she needed to be told.)*
That's a C-A-R-O-U-S-E-L, Honey! Isn't it pretty?
And the music is called C-A-L-L-I-O-P-E music,
like the kind you heard at the circus!
Remember when you saw the big elephant that time?
Oooh, yes, look at the horseys!,"
as she points in continued, gaping amazement.

She hears him, but only as a faraway voice,
too faint to wrest her attention away
from, from — CARE OF SEL
and its
KAL OF PEAS music,
as it continues to swirl and beckon
and fly up and down and sing a song
that vibrates her very marrow
with the purest possible distillate of joy
and color and motion.

She'll carry this event with her her entire life,
whether she dies next year, victim, perhaps,
of some pernicious childhood disease or drunken driver,
or she lives ten decades
and one day takes children of her own
to see this bellicose, noisy miracle,
and attempts,
against the rules,
to experience again the instant she first saw it,
even though she'll never succeed.
It simply isn't allowed.

And through some impossible act of grace,
the only people at the waterfront
that perfect summer's evening
were the little girl with her parents
and you and me.

Wordlessly, we watched this movie unfold,
moved to the brink of tears by the raw,
honest, paralyzing, hopeless,
all-consuming rapture of the little girl,
understanding we'd likely never again bear witness
to such pure, unrefined happiness in our lives.

We carried that memory with us for decades,
sharing it with friends,
and between ourselves,
at times to amplify our joy,
at others to lighten our sorrow.

Now I carry that memory alone,
now that I understand that all of life's joy
harbors the promise of even greater pain,
the experience of the first always mortgaged
against the latter.

I feel both in heartbreaking measure
when I remember that night,
and I ache with gratitude to have shared
that moment with you,
while I choke on my tears,
knowing I'll never again say to you,
"Honey, remember the carousel by the beach?,"
never see your face alight with the memory,
watch your radiant smile appear as you recall
the dusk, the lights, the music,
and the ecstasy of a little girl's
first encounter with magic,
and understand I'll never be that happy again,
in life or memory.
It simply isn't permitted.

— Memorial Day Weekend, 2020

# all aboard

What are we bound to tolerate
when loss leads to life we'd prefer to escape?
All clear the slate, what difference the date,
a few crumbs of existence left on the plate?

A species convinced of its own significance,
at its base composed of identical elements
as anemones and asparagus, equines and elephants,
mere top-of-the-food-chain, self-dealing sycophants.

Are we obliged to await our mother's Trinity
to arrange final passage on to infinity,
so concerned for our mortal virginity
we quail at the tariff if we depart the vicinity?

Loneliness and boredom, twin infiltrates,
give cause to consider departure dates,
whether sailing to heaven on silver skates,
or slithering to hell through warmer gates.

It’s less than a toss-up, but more than a gamble,
whether life is the end or just the preamble,
so is it pack a valise and exit the scramble,
or grab for the ring at the end of the dangle?

In the end it’s the end, whether sine or cosine,
and the worst of the best is better than fine,
so the hedge lets the conductor signal the time
and endures the caboose to the end of the line.

— 4/29/20

# afterword

I'd like to share a few personal thoughts on grieving, based solely on my experience.

There's no one way to grieve. Everyone's experience is going to be unique to them, based on their situation, their loss, and a host of other factors. We may all experience some common emotions, but how they appear, when they leave, in what order they occur, and a million other things are going to be something only you experience. I'm not big on the "stages" theory, only because I think it's largely misinterpreted as a formula. Grief doesn't work that way, in my experience. It's freeform and not easily constrained, and it's going to take you where it wants to go. Sometimes that's where you need to go, and others, it most definitely is not.

There's no "clock" on grieving. One of the most eye-opening moments for me came in my very first session with a therapist, several months after my wife had passed. They asked why I'd come to see them, and I explained, through tears, that my wife had died, and I wasn't handling it very well, to which they replied, "How should you be handling it?" As obvious as it seems in retrospect, I was working to some expectation of how long and how intensely I "should have" been grieving, and internally criticizing myself for it. The timeline is going to be different for everyone. No one can tell you how long you'll grieve or how long you "should" grieve. In my case, I needed someone to tell me I had permission to grieve in any way I needed to, as long as I needed to, and keep me between the guardrails while I did so.

On that topic, my experience is that there's an expectation, not only that you'll "move on," but that you *should* "move on" after an "appropriate" period of time, which seems, in our culture, to be about a year, more or less. I actually had an acquaintance ask me, six months after my wife of nearly forty years had passed, if I "...(had) a new girlfriend yet," proffered with an invitation to bring this presumptive new partner to dinner at their home — a statement and offer I found at once stunning and deeply offensive. Another, a few months later, asked me if I was "still sad," a question that brought me to tears on the spot. Does that question even have an answer, much less a "right" answer? (Yes, I am still sad, even today.)

People are going to say some surprising things to you. Some of them ridiculous, some offensive, some painful, even. I've tried very hard, at least if not in the moment, but over time, to understand that no one likely sets out to say something hurtful to you. Death and its personal impact is one of the most omnipresent but least discussed aspects of our experience as humans. It's going to happen to people we know and love and it's going to happen to us. Yet it makes most of us incredibly uncomfortable, and because we have so little experience discussing it, most of us aren't good at it. So if you're new to grieving, brace yourself. You will hear some stunningly insensitive things if my experience is any guide. By and large, I believe the speaker doesn't mean them that way, and I think in the majority of cases, would be personally horrified and embarrassed to understand what you heard them say.

There are different kinds of grief. Prior to losing my wife, I had lost both of my siblings, my older sister and older brother, then my mother, and finally my father. I grieved them all, deeply, and I thought I understood the impact of grief, the course of it, how to live with it. I was wrong about that, horribly, horribly wrong. None of those losses prepared me in virtually any way for the loss of my wife, my partner, my lover, my best friend, of nearly forty years. The situation was and is orders of magnitude different from my prior experiences, and it remains so to this day.

You may need some help, and there is absolutely no shame in that. Several months after my wife's passing, I approached my primary care physician for an antidepressant. This was contrary to my every extinct, but I simply felt worse than I could deal with on my own. He agreed with my request, but suggested that talk therapy combined with an antidepressant was proven to be much more effective in combination to deal with depression, and suggested a therapist. Reluctantly, I made an appointment. Reluctant, because, among other things, I'm a man, and I'm supposed to be able to take care of myself, not to mention everyone I care about. ("It's just a compound fracture, walk it off and quitcher' whinin'! Time to cowboy up!") So in addition to my grief, I felt a certain amount of shame about my grief, or at least in exposing it to others, even though I needed to very badly. So I went to therapy, and thank goodness I did.

For me, at least, having someone to talk to was critical.

My nuclear family was all gone, and yes, I have close friends I talked with and continue to talk with, including some who had lost their spouses, but none of them are trained mental health professionals. And while all were willing and sympathetic, it's simply not their job, especially over an extended period of time.

One of the most helpful things about therapy, for me, is that long after I would have worn my friends to a nub, my therapist is still there for me, still willing to listen, and with an objective view of me and my situation. It's not a process of breakthrough after breakthrough — it's a process of lots and lots and lots of talk, lots of thinking between those talks, and incremental adjustment, the phrase I use in lieu of the word "improvement." For me, and again, it will be different for anyone else, this process has been almost entirely about learning how to think about and live with the unthinkable and the unlivable.

And then, of course, there's this book. As I explained at the outset, the first poem came from something my therapist said about living in a "world of wrong." The idea to assemble these poems into a book was theirs as well, very early on, when I had fallen into the habit of bringing one or more new poems to each session to serve as a summary, of sorts, of how I had been feeling since our last appointment, and to express emotions I doubt I could have even put into words at the time of any given meeting.

So should everyone write poems? Of course not. (If you've made it this far you may be thinking, "He shouldn't have written poems!") But I'd encourage some form of personal expression, whether it's a diary, a journal, photographs, music, a scrapbook, quilt, paintings, drawings, voice memos, etc., if for no other reason that, as humans, we're horrible at multi-tasking (i.e., we can't hold many thoughts in our head at one time, and we actually have pretty poor memories in general.) Had I not found a way to capture a lot of these feelings, I wouldn't have this record or the opportunity to review my progress, such as it is. Reading my own poems, I can't remember how I came to write some of them, and I'm convinced that I couldn't recompose the vast majority of them today because the emotional state I was in when I composed any given one has passed. As a single example, one lonely Saturday night, apropos of nothing I could identify, I became increasingly angry. Angry to the point of rage. The product of that rage was "Satisfaction." I haven't had a moment quite like that since.

So that's it. There may be some more poems, or maybe not. When I got to the last one that appears here, I knew it was the last one, at least for this book. My wife was an amazing woman, and led an amazing life, so maybe there's a book there somewhere that needs me to write it. I don't know. But this is a journey with no defined end point, so for now it continues to be just one foot in front of the other. If you've read this far, I hope this has helped you. If it has, I thank you for that.

G. Greene

P.S. — This book was started before the arrival of the COVID-19 pandemic in late 2019/early 2020. It was finished in early May 2020, before the virus reached its peak in the United States.

I spent seven months by my wife's side, every day, as she succumbed to the unknown illness that killed her. In the last week, I was by her side twenty-four hours a day, and I was with her, as was her family, at the moment she died. As impossible as that was, I simply can neither imagine nor fathom the pain of those who have lost loved ones during the pandemic and were denied the chance to be beside them. The pain of grief is enough to bear without the additional burden of not being there to say goodbye. If you've been through that experience I am so sorry for your loss and what you and your loved one had to endure. For what it's worth, and I don't expect it's much, it wasn't your fault. Please be kind to yourself. I wish you peace.